The 50 Useful Excel Functions Quiz Book

M.L. HUMPHREY

TITLES BY M.L. HUMPHREY

EXCEL ESSENTIALS
Excel for Beginners
Intermediate Excel
50 Useful Excel Functions
50 More Excel Functions

EXCEL ESSENTIALS QUIZ BOOKS
The Excel for Beginners Quiz Book
The Intermediate Excel Quiz Book
The 50 Useful Excel Functions Quiz Book
The 50 More Excel Functions Quiz Book

DATA PRINCIPLES
Data Principles for Beginners

EASY EXCEL ESSENTIALS
Pivot Tables
Conditional Formatting
Charts
The IF Functions
Formatting
Printing

WORD ESSENTIALS
Word for Beginners
Intermediate Word

MAIL MERGE
Mail Merge for Beginners

POWERPOINT ESSENTIALS
PowerPoint for Beginners

BUDGETING FOR BEGINNERS
Budgeting for Beginners
Excel for Budgeting

CONTENTS

INTRODUCTION

This is a companion book written to complement *50 Useful Excel Functions* by M.L. Humphrey and is geared towards those who are already familiar with the functions covered in that book who now want to test their knowledge through quizzes or to those who learn better from a question and answer format.

The quizzes in this book are in the same order as in *50 Useful Excel Functions* but are sometimes grouped by related functions. So one quiz might cover, for example, functions related to basic math.

The first section of the book just has the questions, the next section of the book has the questions as well as the answers. There is also a bonus section that contains five exercises where you can test your knowledge of the various functions by applying them to specific real-life scenarios.

I encourage you to try to do each exercise first without looking at the solutions, since in the real world you'll be faced with a problem that needs solved and no one will be there to tell you which functions to use. However, I would also encourage you to have Excel open as you work each exercise so you can use the help functions within Excel to find the functions you need. Don't feel like you need to memorize every function in Excel in order to use it effectively. You just need to know what's possible and then what keywords or phrasing to use to help you find the right function.

Finally, both *50 Useful Excel Functions* and *50 More Excel Functions* cover the same basic information about how formulas and functions work so there is overlap in the quizzes for each book. If you've already read *The 50 More Excel Functions Quiz Book*, then you can skip those quizzes because they're identical to the ones contained in that book.

Alright, then. Let's start with the first quiz.

QUIZZES

HOW FORMULAS AND FUNCTIONS WORK QUIZ

1. If you're writing a basic formula in Excel, what symbols can you use to indicate this to Excel?

2. If you're starting a formula using a function in Excel, which symbol do you need to use to indicate this to Excel?

3. If you enter a formula in Excel and then hit enter, what are you going to see in that cell in your worksheet?

4. If you want to see the actual formula that's in a cell, how can you do that?

5. What is the difference between a formula and a function?

6. What are the symbols you can use for adding, subtracting, multiplying, or dividing in Excel?

7. What do the following formulas do?

    A. =3+2

    B. =3-2

    C. =3*2

    D. =3/2

    E. =4+(3*2)

    F. =(4+3)*2

8. What do the following formulas do?

    A. =A1+C1

    B. =A1-C1

    C. =A1*C1

    D. =A1/C1

    E. =E1+(A1*C1)

    F. =(E1+A1)*C1

9. What do examples E and F of the last two questions above demonstrate?

10. What's a best practice when building a really complex formula in Excel?

11. How do you write a function in Excel when it's at the beginning of a formula?

12. Can you use more than once function within a single cell in Excel?

13. What happens if you give the wrong cell range for your function?

WHERE TO FINDFUNCTIONS QUIZ

1. In newer versions of Excel where can you go to look for a function to perform a specific task?

2. What are the categories of functions available in Excel?

3. If you bring up the Insert Function dialogue box and are looking to perform a specific task with a function, where can you search for that?

4. What happens when you click on a function name under Select a Function in the Insert Function dialogue box?

5. If that's not enough information, what can you do?

6. What happens when you select a function from the Insert Function dialogue box?

7. If you already know the function you want to use, but aren't sure of the inputs or the order they need to be entered in, what can you do within your Excel worksheet?

8. If you click on the function name after you've typed, =FUNCTION_NAME(what will you get?

9. What if you still can't figure out what function to use to do what you want to do or don't even know if a function exists for what you're looking to do?

10. What can you do if you're using a version of Excel that's prior to Excel 2007 and so don't have a Formulas tab to go to but want to bring up the Insert Function dialogue box?

FORMULA AND FUNCTION BEST PRACTICES QUIZ

1. Name four best practices when working with formulas or functions.

2. Explain what it means to make your assumptions visible.

3. Explain what it means to use paste special-values when you're done with your calculations and when you should not do this.

4. How can you paste special-values to replace a formula with just the result of the formula?

5. Explain why you should store your raw data in one location and work on a copy of that data instead.

6. What's another best practice when doing a lot of complex work with a dataset that requires multiple steps and manipulations?

7. Why should you test your formulas before applying them to a large data set?

8. Why can't you just accept the results Excel gives you? Why should you always "gut check" those results?

COPYING FORMULAS QUIZ

1. What happens when you copy a formula from one cell to another?

2. If you write a formula and you want to fix the reference to a specific cell so that even if the formula is copied elsewhere it continues to reference that cell, how can you do this?

3. What if you just want to lock the row reference but not the entire cell reference?

4. What if you just want to lock the column reference but not the entire cell reference?

5. If you just want to move a formula to a new location without it changing, what's the best way to do that?

BASIC MATH FUNCTIONS QUIZ

1. What is the function you can use to sum a range of values or a range of cells?

2. How would you write a function to sum the values in Column A?

3. How would you write a function to sum the values in Rows 1 through 3?

4. How would you write a function to sum the values in Columns A, C, and E?

5. How would you write a function to sum the values in Cells A1 through B6?

6. How would you write a function to subtract the total of all customer orders in Column C from the amount collected which is listed in Cell F1?

7. What is the function you can use to multiply a range of values or a range of cells?

8. If you want to multiply number of units in Cell A1 times unit price in Cell B1 times tax rate in Cell C1, how would you write that using a function?

9. What is another way to do that that doesn't use a function?

10. What is the function you can use to multiply a range of values and then sum those results?

11. What are the inputs that go into that function?

12. If you have a table with number of units in Column A and unit price in Column B and you want to calculate the total earned (units times price and then summed across all rows), how would you write that using a single function?

13. What's another way to do that calculation?

14. When using SUMPRODUCT, what does the #VALUE! error message likely indicate?

15. What does Excel do with text entries that are included in a SUMPRODUCT cell range?

16. Can you use SUMPRODUCT for rows of data instead of columns?

17. Is there a function for subtracting values from one another?

18. Is there a function for dividing values by one another?

19. Why?

20. If you have a series of a hundred numbers in Column B that you want to subtract from the value in Cell A1, how can you use a function to do that?

AVERAGES, MEANS, AND MODES QUIZ

1. What is the difference between an average, a mean, and a mode?

2. What's a good idea when dealing with a large range of data points that will help you figure out whether average, mean, or mode works best for your data?

3. If I want to calculate the average of values in Cells A1 through A5, how can I do that using a function?

4. What happens if one of the cells in that range is blank?

5. What can you do to make sure that Excel includes all cells within the specified range when using the AVERAGE function?

6. What happens if one of the cells in that range contains text?

7. What can you do to make sure that Excel includes cells

with text in them when calculating an average over a range of cells?

8. Can you take an average of the returns of a TRUE/FALSE series of responses to get the overall percent of responses that were true? How?

9. If I have four cells with the values 2, 6, Other, and Now, what result will I get using AVERAGE? What result will I get using AVERAGEA?

10. How does AVERAGEA handle blank cells in a range?

11. How would you write the function to calculate the median of a range of values from Cells C1 through C9?

12. How does Excel calculate the median when there is an even number of values in the range?

13. Why can this be dangerous?

14. Can you use median with TRUE/FALSE values?

15. What's a way to work around the need to type the TRUE and FALSE into the function itself?

16. What function should you use to find the most common result when your data has a large bump that isn't near the midline?

17. How would you write this function for a range of values in Cells B2 through B10?

18. What does MODE.MULT let you do?

19. What is special about the MODE.MULT function?

20. How do you use MODE.MULT?

21. If you've properly used MODE.MULT, what will it look like in the formula bar when you click back into the cell for the function?

22. If you have multi-modal data where two values occur with the same high frequency but you use the MODE.SNGL or MODE function instead of the MODE.MULT function, what will happen?

23. What can you do if you want your MODE.MULT results to display in a row instead of in a column?

24. What is one issue with MODE.MULT that you're still going to run into?

25. How could you work around this issue?

MINIMUMS AND MAXIMUMS QUIZ

1. If you want the minimum value within a range, what function can you use to get it?

2. If you want the maximum value within a range, what function can you use to get it?

3. How would you write the function to calculate the minimum value in Column D?

4. How would you write the function to calculate the maximum value in Row 3?

5. What value will Excel return if you ask for the minimum or maximum of a range of values that have no numbers in them?

6. What will happen if you try to take the minimum or maximum of a range of values that has an error value in it such as #DIV/0!?

7. If you have a range of values that you want to take a minimum of but that range includes TRUE and FALSE

entries that you want included in the calculation, what function should you use?

8. How do MINA and MAXA treat TRUE or FALSE values?

9. How do MINA and MAXA treat text?

10. What result will you get from =MINA(A1:A3) where A1 is the word Other, A2 is 2, and A3 is 3?

11. What result will you get from =MINA(A1:A3) where A1 is -2, A2 is 2, and A3 is 3?

12. What result will you get from =MAXA(A1:A3) where A1 is -2, A2 is 2, and A3 is 3?

ROUNDING QUIZ

1. What functions can you use to round numbers?

2. If you want to round a number to a specified number of digits and it can either be rounded up or down depending on which number it's closest to, which function should you use?

3. If you want to round a number to a specified number of digits and you want to always round away from zero, which function should you use?

4. If you want to round a number to a specified number of digits and you want to always round towards zero, which function should you use?

5. What is the difference between using one of the rounding functions and just formatting a number to display a certain number of decimal places?

6. If you want to round the number 234.561 to the nearest whole number, how would you write that function?

M.L. HUMPHREY

7. What if you wanted to round it to one decimal place?

8. What if you wanted to round it to two decimal places?

9. What if you wanted to round it to the nearest 100's (so 200)?

10. If I tell Excel to round a number to the nearest four decimal places, but there are only two decimal places in the number now, what will Excel do?

11. How does Excel decide with the ROUND function whether to round up or to round down?

12. If you use the ROUNDUP function to round to the nearest two decimal places for 1.239, what will you get?

13. If you use the ROUNDDOWN function to round to the nearest two decimal places for 1.239, what will you get?

14. If you use the ROUNDUP function to round to the nearest two decimal places for 1.231, what will you get?

15. If you use the ROUNDDOWN function to round to the nearest two decimal places for 1.231, what will you get?

16. If you use the ROUNDUP function to round to the nearest two decimal places for -1.239, what will you get?

17. If you use the ROUNDDOWN function to round to the nearest two decimal places for -1.239, what will you get?

18. If you use the ROUNDUP function to round to the nearest two decimal places for -1.231, what will you get?

19. If you use the ROUNDDOWN function to round to the nearest two decimal places for -1.231, what will you get?

20. What issue can you run into if you use ROUNDUP or ROUNDDOWN instead of ROUND?

BASIC COUNT FUNCTIONS QUIZ

1. What does the COUNT function allow you to do?

2. Does COUNT include cells with text in them?

3. Does COUNT include cells with formulas in them that create a number or date?

4. Does COUNT include cells with formulas in them that create a text entry?

5. If a cell contains "1 unit" as its value, will COUNT count it?

6. How would you use COUNT on a range of cells from B2 through D8?

7. What function can you use if you also want to count cells that contain text in them?

8. What does this function allow you to do?

9. What happens when you have a function in a cell, say

=CONCATENATE(A1,B1,C1) but that cell is currently not displaying a value and you use each of the count functions?

10. What should you always do when using any function?

11. What does COUNTBLANK do?

12. If you have an issue with which cells are being counted by a specific count function, what should you do?

THE COUNTIFS, SUMIFS, AND AVERAGEIFS FUNCTIONS QUIZ

1. What is the difference between COUNTIFS, SUMIFS, and AVERAGEIFS?

2. If you have access to both COUNTIF and COUNTIFS (or both SUMIF and SUMIFS, or both AVERAGEIF and AVERAGEIFS), which one should you use? Why?

3. What is the difference between COUNTIF and COUNTIFS? What about SUMIF and SUMIFS? And AVERAGEIF and AVERAGEIFS?

4. If you want to count how many times the values in Cells C10 through C25 are the same as the value in Cell A1, how would you write that function?

5. What if you wanted to count how many times the cells in that range had text that included an e in it?

6. Could you count how many cells from Cells C10 through C25 have the same values as Cell A1 AND how

many have an e in them? If so, how would you write that and what issue would you potentially run into?

7. If you want to count how many times the values in Cells C10 through C25 are greater than the value in Cell A1, how would you write that?

8. If you want to count how many customers are from Alaska and have bought Widgets when your customer location is stored in Column C and your product is stored in Column E, how would you write that?

9. If you want to count how many customers have bought more than 10 of your product and are from Hawaii when customer location is stored in Column C and number of units is in Column D, how would you write that?

10. If you want to count how many times Student A scored over 90 and Student B scored over 90 when their test scores are recorded in Rows 2 and 3, how would you do that?

11. What do you need to watch out for when using COUNTIFS, SUMIFS, and AVERAGEIFS?

12. If you want to total the value of all customer orders, which is listed in Column H, for all customers from Maine, which is listed in Column C, and who bought Widgets, which is listed in Column E, how would you do that?

13. Can you total the value of all customer orders over $100 using SUMIF or SUMIFS? How would you write that assuming customer order value is listed in Column H?

14. What do the asterisk (*), the question mark (?), and the tilde (~) represent when you're writing a count, sum, or average criteria?

15. Can you calculate the average customer order for a customer in Colorado who made a purchase in June, assuming that customer order is stored in Column H, customer location is in Column C, and purchase month is in Column B? How would you write that?

16. If there are no customer transactions that meet that criteria what result is Excel going to return?

17. With COUNTIFS, SUMIFS, and AVERAGEIFS, if you have three criteria you specify and two of the three are met, what will happen with that entry?

18. Why is this important?

BASIC TEXT
FUNCTIONS QUIZ

1. If you want to convert a text string into uppercase letters, which function should you use?

2. What if you want to convert a text string into lowercase letters?

3. What if you want the initial letter of each word to be capitalized, but the rest to be in lowercase?

4. Let's say that you have a text string in Cell C10 and another in Cell C11 and that you want to combine those entries with a space between them and convert them into uppercase letters. How could you do that?

5. What does CONCATENATE do?

6. What is the difference between proper case and title case?

7. What does the LEFT function do?

8. If you want to return the first five characters of the text in Cell A1, how would you do that?

9. Does this function work with numbers as well?

10. What happens if the number of characters you specify is greater than the number of characters in the string you reference?

11. What happens if you don't specify a number of characters to return?

12. For languages that don't work with characters, like Chinese, Japanese, and Korean, which function will do the same for those languages?

13. If you want to return the last two characters of a text string, how can you do that?

14. What does the MID function do?

15. What happens if the start point you provide for the MID function is greater than the number of characters in the string?

16. What happens if you use MID and ask Excel to return more characters than there are in the text string?

17. What other function could you use to get the same result as =MID(A1,1,2)?

18. If you want to take a text string and remove all spaces from it except for one space between each word, which function can you use to do that?

19. If you had a list of entries with first name, middle name, and last name in separate columns, Columns A, B,

and C, and you wanted to combine those entries for each row into one entry with only one space between each word, and you knew that not every entry had a middle name, how could you use two functions to do that in one cell? Write the function for Row 1.

20. What do you need to be careful of when using any of the above functions? What can you do when you're done with your manipulation to address this?

21. What type of inputs will CONCATENATE accept? And how do they need to be written?

22. If you want there to be a space or a comma in your final CONCATENATE result, how do you do that?

23. With CONCATENATE if you get a NAME#? error, what has generally gone wrong?

24. What function is Excel replacing CONCATENATE with?

THE TEXT FUNCTION QUIZ

1. What does Excel say that the TEXT function can do?

2. What else can the TEXT function actually do?

3. If you have a date in Cell A1 and want to pull the full name of the day of the week, how would you do that using the TEXT function?

4. What about the month of the year?

5. If you use TEXT to create number formats, for example =TEXT(A1,"$0.00"), what issue can you run into?

6. What is the other thing to be aware of when using the TEXT function with a number?

7. What's one quick way to see valid number formats you can use with the TEXT function?

8. If you wanted to return the number value in Cell A1 as "50% Win Rate", how could you do that using TEXT?

THE TODAY AND NOW FUNCTIONS QUIZ

1. What does the TODAY function do?

2. How do you write it?

3. Why would you use it?

4. If you wanted to calculate how many days it's been since someone purchased your product, which is the better option: have a cell that uses =TODAY() and then another cell that calculates days since purchase or just have a cell that calculates days since purchase and incorporates TODAY() into the formula? Why?

5. What does the NOW function do?

6. What's the difference between using TODAY and NOW?

7. Why does this matter?

8. What do you need to be aware of when using both TODAY and NOW?

9. How does Excel treat dates for the purpose of addition and subtraction?

10. So if you wanted to calculate the date five and a half days from today's date, what could you use?

11. What if you wanted to calculate the date and time exactly five and a half days from this moment?

12. Is it possible that those two formulas could return different dates?

THE IF FUNCTION QUIZ

1. What does an IF function do?

2. Translate the IF function =IF(A2>25,0,A2*0.05) into a written description.

3. What is another way to think about the components of an IF function?

4. What does it mean that you can nest IF functions?

5. If you're going to nest IF functions, which is it better to replace, the Then portion or the Else portion? Why?

6. Translate the IF function =IF(A9>$A$5,$B$5,IF(A9>$A$4,$B$4,0)) into a written description.

7. If you were to copy the above formula into a new cell, how would it change?

8. If you have a long and complex nested IF function that you can't get to work, what are some ways you can troubleshoot the IF function to figure out what's wrong?

9. What is the most likely issue if Excel tells you you've entered too many arguments with an IF function?

10. What should you always do with an IF function that you create? (Or any function really?)

11. If you write an IF function that's referencing a table of fixed values (like a discount table) what should you always be sure to do?

VLOOKUP QUIZ

1. What does VLOOKUP do?

2. What must you do if you're using VLOOKUP on a table?

3. What's the best use for VLOOKUP?

4. Do the values in a reference table need to be an exact match for the value you're looking for for VLOOKUP to work?

5. What is the minimum number of columns your data needs for VLOOKUP to work?

6. Can the column that has the values you're looking up be located anywhere in your data?

7. How do you tell Excel whether to look for an exact match or an approximate match?

8. What is the difference between an exact match and an approximate match?

9. What is =VLOOKUP(25,A1:E10,3,FALSE) saying to do?

10. What is =VLOOKUP(25,A1:E10,2,TRUE) saying to do?

11. What do you need to be careful of when using VLOOKUP with apparent numbers or dates?

12. What should you always do when using any function in Excel?

THE AND & OR FUNCTIONS QUIZ

1. What does the AND function do?

2. What does the OR function do?

3. What is =AND(A1>5,A2>4) asking?

4. What is =OR(A1>5,A2>4) asking?

5. What is =AND(A1>B1,A2>B2) asking?

6. What is =IF(AND(A1="Jones",B1="Whatsit"),C1,D1) doing?

7. What is =IF(OR(A1="Canton",B1="Toledo"),G1,G1*2) doing?

THE TRUE, FALSE AND NA FUNCTIONS QUIZ

1. What do the TRUE and FALSE functions do?

2. When might you use them?

3. What does the NA function do?

4. When might you use the NA function?

5. What do you need to remember when using the TRUE, FALSE, or NA functions?

RANDOM NUMBERS QUIZ

1. What function will return a random number greater than or equal to 0 and less than 1 evenly distributed?

2. What function will return a random whole number between two values you specify?

3. If I want to return any possible value, including a decimal value between 0 and 100, how can I do that?

4. If I want to return any whole number between 0 and 100, how can I do that?

5. What do you need to be careful of when using either function?

6. How can you work around this if you need to capture that value?

RANKING QUIZ

1. What function or functions can you use if you want to know the rank of a specific value within a range of possible values? In other words, is this the 5th largest number, the 10th, the 20th, etc. compared to other numbers in the range?

2. If you want to know the rank of a value in Cell A1 from within the range of Cells A1 through A15, how can you write that function using ascending values?

3. What about using descending values?

4. To use the functions does your data have to be sorted?

5. What happens if you use RANK on a data set where there are multiples of a value?

6. How do RANK.EQ and RANK.AVG differ?

THE SMALL AND LARGE FUNCTIONS QUIZ

1. What does the SMALL function do?

2. What does the LARGE function do?

3. Can you technically use SMALL to return the largest value in a range and LARGE to return the smallest value in a range?

4. What does the ROWS function do?

COMBINING FUNCTIONS QUIZ

1. Is it possible to write a formula that uses more than one function?

2. How would you write a formula that returns a value of TRUE if the value in Cell A1 is greater than 10 or the value in Cell B1 is greater than 10 and a value of FALSE otherwise?

3. What do you need to be careful about when combining functions together in one formula?

4. Do you need to use an equals sign in front of each function name when you combine functions in a single formula?

5. What should you explore further if you're running into file size issues because of repeat calculations in your Excel worksheet?

WHEN THINGS GO
WRONG QUIZ

1. Name five different error messages you might see.

2. What does #REF! generally indicate?

3. How can you see where the cell that was deleted was located in your formula?

4. What does a #VALUE! message indicate?

5. What does a #DIV/0! message indicate?

6. If the #DIV/0! message is legitimate because nothing has been entered yet, what's a quick way to suppress it?

7. What does a #N/A error message generally mean?

8. What can you check for if this happens and you don't think it should have?

9. What does the IFERROR function do? What do you need to be careful with if you use it?

10. What does the #NUM! error message generally indicate?

11. What is a circular reference?

12. If you don't think you have a circular reference but Excel tells you you do, what should you check for?

13. If you're trying to figure out what cells are feeding the value in a cell where can you go to do that?

14. If Excel tells you you have too few arguments, what should you check for?

15. What can you do with a formula that just isn't working the way it should be?

CELL NOTATION QUIZ

1. What is Cell A1 referencing?

2. Name two ways you can reference more than one cell in a function.

3. Can you reference a cell in another worksheet?

4. Can you reference a cell in another workbook?

5. What's an easy way to reference a cell in another worksheet or workbook?

QUIZ ANSWERS

HOW FORMULAS AND FUNCTIONS WORK QUIZ ANSWERS

1. If you're writing a basic formula in Excel, what symbols can you use to indicate this to Excel?

You can use a plus sign (+), a minus sign (-), or an equals sign (=).

2. If you're starting a formula using a function in Excel, which symbol do you need to use to indicate this to Excel?

The equals sign (=).

3. If you enter a formula in Excel and then hit enter, what are you going to see in that cell in your worksheet?

The result. So, for example, if you type =2+2 into a cell and hit enter you will see 4, the result of adding two plus two, in the cell where you entered the formula.

4. If you want to see the actual formula that's in a cell, how can you do that?

Click on the cell and look in the formula bar or double-click on the cell to see the formula in the cell itself.

5. What is the difference between a formula and a function?

A function lets you perform a specified task. It's like a programmed shortcut. That task can be mathematical (like SUM) or it can be related to text (like CONCATENATE), dates, or logic. A formula is a way of performing a calculation using Excel and it can not only involve functions but also just basic math notation.

6. What are the symbols you can use for adding, subtracting, multiplying, or dividing in Excel?

To add you can use the plus sign (+). To subtract you can use the minus sign (-). To multiply you can use the asterisk (*). And to divide you can use the forward slash (/).

7. What do the following formulas do?

A. =3+2

Adds 3 to 2

B. =3-2

Subtracts 2 from 3

C. =3*2

Multiplies 3 by 2

D. =3/2

Divides 3 by 2

E. =4+(3*2)

Multiplies 3 by 2 and then adds the result to 4

F. =(4+3)*2

Adds 4 to 3 and then multiplies the result by 2

8. What do the following formulas do?
A. =A1+C1

Adds the value in A1 to the value in C1

B. =A1-C1
Subtracts the value in C1 from the value in A1

C. =A1*C1
Multiplies the value in A1 by the value in C1

D. =A1/C1
Divides the value in A1 by the value in C1

E. =E1+(A1*C1)
Multiplies the value in A1 by the value in C1 and then adds the result to the value in E1

F. =(E1+A1)*C1
Adds the value in E1 to the value in A1 and then multiplies the result by the value in C1

9. What do examples E and F from the last two questions above demonstrate?

How important it is when writing a complex formula that you place your parens in the right place, because that will determine the order in which Excel performs its calculations and will impact your answer.

10. What's a best practice when building a really complex formula in Excel?

Build it in pieces and test that each piece is calculating correctly before combining all of the pieces together.

11. How do you write a function in Excel when it's at the beginning of a formula?

=FUNCTION_NAME(
You start with an equals sign, follow that with the function name, and then immediately follow that with an opening paren.

12. Can you use more than once function within a single cell in Excel?

Yes.

13. What happens if you give the wrong cell range for your function?

Garbage in, garbage out. It won't do what you want it to do. For a function to properly work it needs to be the right one and you need to give it the right inputs in the right order.

WHERE TO FIND FUNCTIONS
QUIZ ANSWERS

1. In newer versions of Excel where can you go to look for a function to perform a specific task?

The Formulas tab will show you a Function Library set of dropdowns arranged by type (Financial, Logical, Text, etc.) and you can hold your mouse over each one for a brief description of what it does. But if you don't know the function you want, it's better to go to Insert Function and bring up the Insert Function dialogue box. This will let you search using a few keywords for the function you want.

2. What are the categories of functions available in Excel?

Financial, Logical, Text, Date & Time, Lookup & Reference, Math & Trig, Statistical, Engineering, Cube, Information, Compatibility, Web

3. If you bring up the Insert Function dialogue box and are looking to perform a specific task with a function, where can you search for that?

In the Search For a Function box at the top. Enter a few keywords related to what you want to do and then click on Go. Excel will list functions in the Select a Function box that meet those keywords.

4. What happens when you click on a function name under Select a Function in the Insert Function dialogue box?

Excel will show you a brief description of what the function does as well as a sample of what inputs the function requires to work.

5. If that's not enough information, what can you do?

Click on Help on This Function in the bottom left corner.

6. What happens when you select a function from the Insert Function dialogue box?

It brings up the Function Arguments box which will show you the description for the function, a sample output for the function based upon the choices you make, and input boxes for you to add the information required for the function.

7. If you already know the function you want to use, but aren't sure of the inputs or the order they need to be entered in, what can you do within your Excel worksheet?

Type =FUNCTION_NAME to see the Excel description of what the function does. Type =FUNCTION_NAME(to see a list of the inputs for the function and the order in which they need to appear.

8. If you click on the function name after you've typed, =FUNCTION_NAME(what will you get?

An Excel Help dialogue box for that function.

9. What if you still can't figure out what function to use to do what you want to do or don't even know if a

function exists for what you're looking to do?

Do an internet search. Chances are someone else at some point wanted to do the exact same thing you do.

10. What can you do if you're using a version of Excel that's prior to Excel 2007 and so don't have a Formulas tab to go to but want to bring up the Insert Function dialogue box?

Type an equals sign into a cell, go to the white dropdown box to the left of the formula bar, click on the dropdown arrow, and choose More Functions from the bottom of the list.

FORMULA AND FUNCTION BEST PRACTICES QUIZ ANSWERS

1. Name four best practices when working with formulas or functions.

Make your assumptions visible, use paste special-values when you're done with your calculations, store your raw data in one location and work on a copy of that data for any calculations or manipulations, test your formulas to make sure they work under all possible circumstances especially threshold cases.

2. Explain what it means to make your assumptions visible.

While it's possible to write a formula that has all of the information written within a cell, it's better to show on your worksheet any inputs into that formula. For example, if I assume that selling my house is going to cost me 3% in realtor fees, it's better to have a field in Excel for realtor fees that I can see at a glance and to reference that cell with my formula than to build that 3% amount into a formula where I'll only see it if I click on that cell. (Especially since that number is very likely wrong.)

3. Explain what it means to use paste special-values when you're done with your calculations and when you should not do this.

Do not do this if you expect to update your information that's feeding the calculation. This should only be done when you are completely finished with your analysis. Because if you do it and then update an input into the formula, the formula no longer exists and your final answer will not update with the new information.

But the reason to do this is the same. If you've finished your calculation using paste special-values will lock in your results so that they can't be impacted by deleting data that was used to make the calculation.

4. How can you paste special-values to replace a formula with just the result of the formula?

Click on the cell with formula and Copy (Ctrl +C is the easiest way to do this), right-click on the same cell, and choose to Paste Special and then the Values option from the dropdown menu. (It's the one with the 123 on the clipboard.)

5. Explain why you should store your raw data in one location and work on a copy of that data instead.

Because some things can't be undone. If you sort only part of your data, for example, and don't realize it until later your entire dataset will be useless. Or if you find and replace the wrong information. Or you remove duplicates from only part of your data. Etc.

6. What's another best practice when doing a lot of complex work with a dataset that requires multiple steps and manipulations?

Save versions of the data as you go after each significant manipulation is completed. This way if you do mess up at some point along the way you can go back to one of those earlier versions rather than having to start over from scratch.

7. Why should you test your formulas before applying them to a large data set?

To make sure they're working properly, especially at the thresholds. So, for example, if you're using an IF function that returns one value when the value in Column A is over 25 and another value when it's under, you should test what happens when the value in Column A is 25. Is that the result you want? If not, you need to edit the formula. And it's easier to catch these things in test scenarios that are designed to test the edges than in a thousand rows of data.

8. Why can't you just accept the results Excel gives you? Why should you always "gut check" those results?

Because Excel just does what you tell it to do and if you tell it to do the wrong thing it's going to do it without question. So you should always be asking yourself, "does this result make sense"? And if it doesn't, you need to look at the numbers and your result to see if there's an error in your formula.

COPYING FORMULAS
QUIZ ANSWERS

1. What happens when you copy a formula from one cell to another?

All cell references in the formula will adjust based upon the number of rows and columns you moved the formula. So if a formula references Cell A1 and you move it over two columns, that reference to Cell A1 will become a reference to Cell C1. And if you move it down two rows, that reference to Cell A1 will become a reference to Cell A3.

2. If you write a formula and you want to fix the reference to a specific cell so that even if the formula is copied elsewhere it continues to reference that cell, how can you do this?

By using $ signs in front of both the column and row reference. So if you use $A$1 in a formula and copy that formula, the formula will continue to reference Cell A1 no matter where you copy it to.

3. What if you just want to lock the row reference but not the entire cell reference?

Then just put a $ sign in front of the row portion of the cell reference. So, for example, A$1.

4. What if you just want to lock the column reference but not the entire cell reference?

Then just put a $ sign in front of the column portion of the cell reference. So, for example, $A1.

5. If you just want to move a formula to a new location without it changing, what's the best way to do that?

Use Cut instead of Copy. That will move the formula without changing the cell references.

BASIC MATH FUNCTIONS
QUIZ ANSWERS

1. What is the function you can use to sum a range of values or a range of cells?
SUM

2. How would you write a function to sum the values in Column A?
=SUM(A:A)

3. How would you write a function to sum the values in Rows 1 through 3?
=SUM(1:3)

4. How would you write a function to sum the values in Columns A, C, and E?
=SUM(A:A,C:C,E:E)

5. How would you write a function to sum the values in Cells A1 through B6?
=SUM(A1:B6)

6. How would you write a function to subtract the total of all customer orders in Column C from the amount collected which is listed in Cell F1?
=F1-SUM(C:C)

7. What is the function you can use to multiply a range of values or a range of cells?
PRODUCT

8. If you want to multiply number of units in Cell A1 times unit price in Cell B1 times tax rate in Cell C1, how would you write that using a function?
=PRODUCT(A1,B1,C1) or =PRODUCT(A1:C1)

9. What is another way to do that that doesn't use a function?
=A1*B1*C1

10. What is the function you can use to multiply a range of values and then sum those results?
SUMPRODUCT

11. What are the inputs that go into that function?
You tell Excel the range of values that need to be multiplied times one another. So it's written as =SUMPRODUCT(array1, [array2], [array3],...) where each array is a range of cells to be multiplied one entry at a time times the corresponding entry in the other arrays.

12. If you have a table with number of units in Column A and unit price in Column B and you want to calculate the total earned (units times price and then summed across all rows), how would you write that using a single function?
=SUMPRODUCT(A:A,B:B)

13. What's another way to do that calculation?

You could also calculate the product for each row and then sum the total of those results.

14. When using SUMPRODUCT, what does the #VALUE! error message likely indicate?

That the arrays (or cell ranges) that you provided for the function are not the same size.

15. What does Excel do with text entries that are included in a SUMPRODUCT cell range?

Treats the text as a zero which means it will return a zero result for any line where one of the entries is text.

16. Can you use SUMPRODUCT for rows of data instead of columns?

Yes.

17. Is there a function for subtracting values from one another?

No.

18. Is there a function for dividing values by one another?

No.

19. Why?

Because with both subtraction and division the order of the inputs matters. With addition 2+3 and 3+2 give the same result, so you can have a function that adds a range of cells and it will work. But with subtraction 2-3 is not the same as 3-2 so you can't have a function that performs that task. Same with division.

20. If you have a series of a hundred numbers in Column B that you want to subtract from the value in Cell A1, how can you use a function to do that?

=A1-SUM(B:B)

AVERAGES, MEANS, AND MODES
QUIZ ANSWERS

1. What is the difference between an average, a mean, and a mode?

An average is an arithmetic mean of a series of numbers. It's calculated by adding those numbers together and then dividing by the count of the numbers you just added. So if I average 3, 4, and 5, the result is 4 because I add 3, 4, and 5 to get 12 and then divide by 3 to get 4.

The median value is the number in the middle of a range of values. Looking at the example above with 3, 4, and 5 the median value is also 4 because it's the middle value.

But let's change that up. Let's look at 3, 4, and 500 instead of 3, 4, and 5. The average of 3, 4, and 500 is 169 but the median is still 4 because the middle value in that range of numbers is 4. If you have data that is evenly distributed, the two numbers should be similar, but if there's a large skew in your data, then you'll want to look at both results because they could be quite different.

The mode returns the most frequently occurring or repetitive value in a range. It's basically telling you where there's a bump in your data. It's especially useful in situations where there is a heavy concentration of values and that concentration of values is not in the center of the range.

2. What's a good idea when dealing with a large range of data points that will help you figure out whether average, mean, or mode works best for your data?

Plot it. If you put your data points onto a scatter plot you will be able to see if there are any unusual concentrations in the data points or any sort of skew to your data that could impact the result of using average, mean, or mode.

3. If I want to calculate the average of values in Cells A1 through A5, how can I do that using a function?

=AVERAGE(A1:A5)

4. What happens if one of the cells in that range is blank?

Excel will ignore it. So it will sum the other four values and divide by four. It will not divide by five even though there were five cells in our specified range.

5. What can you do to make sure that Excel includes all cells within the specified range when using the AVERAGE function?

Put a zero in any blank cells so that they're included in the calculation.

6. What happens if one of the cells in that range contains text?

Excel will ignore it.

7. What can you do to make sure that Excel includes cells with text in them when calculating an average over a range of cells?

Use the AVERAGEA function instead. It will treat text entries and FALSE values as having a value of 0 and TRUE values as having a value of 1.

8. Can you take an average of the returns of a TRUE/FALSE series of responses to get the overall percent of responses that were true? How?

Yes. Using the AVERAGEA function.

9. If I have four cells with the values 2, 6, Other, and Now, what result will I get using AVERAGE? What result will I get using AVERAGEA?

AVERAGE will return a result of 4 which is 2+6 divided by 2. AVERAGEA will return a result of 2 which is 2+6 divided by 4.

10. How does AVERAGEA handle blank cells in a range?

It ignores them.

11. How would you write the function to calculate the median of a range of values from Cells C1 through C9?

=MEDIAN(C1:C9)

12. How does Excel calculate the median when there is an even number of values in the range?

It averages the middle two values.

13. Why can this be dangerous?

Because if you have data that's something like 1, 1, 100, 100, Excel will return a value of 50.5 even though that value is nowhere close to an actual value in the data.

14. Can you use median with TRUE/FALSE values?

Yes, if they're typed directly into the function. For example, =MEDIAN(TRUE, FALSE, FALSE)

15. What's a way to work around the need to type the TRUE and FALSE into the function itself?

Convert the TRUE/FALSE results into 1s and 0s and then you can reference the numbers using a cell range.

16. What function should you use to find the most common result when your data has a large bump that isn't near the midline?

MODE. Or, in recent versions of Excel, MODE.SNGL or MODE.MULT.

17. How would you write this function for a range of values in Cells B2 through B10?

=MODE(B2:B10) or MODE.SNGL(B2:B10)

18. What does MODE.MULT let you do?

Return more than one result when you have muti-modal data. (Meaning data that has more than one bump to it.)

19. What is special about the MODE.MULT function?

It's an array formula which means it returns results in more than one cell.

20. How do you use MODE.MULT?

Highlight the range of cells where you want Excel to return your results. If there are two bumps in the data, highlight two cells. If there are three, highlight three cells, etc. Only once you've done this should you type in your MODE.MULT function with the cell range you want to evaluate. And then, instead of hitting Enter, you hit Ctrl + Shift + Enter.

21. If you've properly used MODE.MULT, what will it look like in the formula bar when you click back into the cell for the function?

It will have curvy brackets at each end like this: {=MODE.MULT(A1:A10)}

22. If you have multi-modal data where two values occur with the same high frequency but you use the MODE.SNGL or MODE function instead of the MODE.MULT function, what will happen?

Excel will return the first value that occurs at that frequency. So if 5 and 25 both occur at an equally frequent high amount in the data, Excel will only return the 5 value.

23. What can you do if you want your MODE.MULT results to display in a row instead of in a column?

Write the formula as

=TRANSPOSE(MODE.MULT(A1:A10))

instead. The TRANSPOSE will flip the results from going down a column to going across a row.

24. What is one issue with MODE.MULT that you're still going to run into?

It's only going to return the most frequently occurring results. So if you have one value that occurs 10 times, another that occurs 10 times, and a third that occurs 9 times it will only return those first two values even though that third one may also be of interest to you.

25. How could you work around this issue?

Build a count table of your values that counts each value and its number of occurrences and then sort by count to see your top values that way.

MINIMUMS AND MAXIMUMS
QUIZ ANSWERS

1. If you want the minimum value within a range, what function can you use to get it?
MIN or MINA

2. If you want the maximum value within a range, what function can you use to get it?
MAX or MAXA

3. How would you write the function to calculate the minimum value in Column D?
=MIN(D:D) or =MINA(D:D)

4. How would you write the function to calculate the maximum value in Row 3?
=MAX(3:3) or =MAXA(3:3)

5. What value will Excel return if you ask for the minimum or maximum of a range of values that have no numbers in them?
0

6. What will happen if you try to take the minimum or maximum of a range of values that has an error value in it such as #DIV/0!?

It will return the error value.

7. If you have a range of values that you want to take a minimum of but that range includes TRUE and FALSE entries that you want included in the calculation, what function should you use?

MINA

8. How do MINA and MAXA treat TRUE or FALSE values?

TRUE values are treated as a 1. FALSE values are treated as a 0.

9. How do MINA and MAXA treat text?

A text entry is treated as a zero.

10. What result will you get from =MINA(A1:A3) where A1 is the word Other, A2 is 2, and A3 is 3?

0

11. What result will you get from =MINA(A1:A3) where A1 is -2, A2 is 2, and A3 is 3?

-2

12. What result will you get from =MAXA(A1:A3) where A1 is -2, A2 is 2, and A3 is 3?

3

ROUNDING QUIZ ANSWERS

1. What functions can you use to round numbers?
ROUND, ROUNDUP, ROUNDDOWN

2. If you want to round a number to a specified number of digits and it can either be rounded up or down depending on which number it's closest to, which function should you use?
ROUND

3. If you want to round a number to a specified number of digits and you want to always round away from zero, which function should you use?
ROUNDUP

4. If you want to round a number to a specified number of digits and you want to always round towards zero, which function should you use?
ROUNDDOWN

5. What is the difference between using one of the rounding functions and just formatting a number to display a certain number of decimal places?

Formatting the number doesn't change the underlying value of that number. So 1.234 will still be 1.234 even if it looks like it's now just 1. Whereas applying ROUND to that number will change it into the number 1 and will remove the decimal places as if they never existed.

6. If you want to round the number 234.561 to the nearest whole number, how would you write that function?
=ROUND(234.561,0)

7. What if you wanted to round it to one decimal place?
=ROUND(234.561,1)

8. What if you wanted to round it to two decimal places?
=ROUND(234.561,2)

9. What if you wanted to round it to the nearest 100's (so 200)?
=ROUND(234.561,-2)

10. If I tell Excel to round a number to the nearest four decimal places, but there are only two decimal places in the number now, what will Excel do?
It'll leave the number as it is. =ROUND(2.34, 4) will return a value of 2.34.

11. How does Excel decide with the ROUND function whether to round up or to round down?
It looks at the digit one past where you told it to round and uses that to decide whether to round up or down. So if you have 1.2646 and tell Excel to round to two digits it will round down to 1.26 because of the 4 in the third position. It will not round up from the 6 to make the 4 a 5 and then round up from that. Digits from 0 through 4 round down. Digits from 5 through 9 round up.

12. If you use the ROUNDUP function to round to the nearest two decimal places for 1.239, what will you get?
1.24

13. If you use the ROUNDDOWN function to round to the nearest two decimal places for 1.239, what will you get?
1.23

14. If you use the ROUNDUP function to round to the nearest two decimal places for 1.231, what will you get?
1.24

15. If you use the ROUNDDOWN function to round to the nearest two decimal places for 1.231, what will you get?
1.23

16. If you use the ROUNDUP function to round to the nearest two decimal places for -1.239, what will you get?
-1.24

17. If you use the ROUNDDOWN function to round to the nearest two decimal places for -1.239, what will you get?
-1.23

18. If you use the ROUNDUP function to round to the nearest two decimal places for -1.231, what will you get?
-1.24

19. If you use the ROUNDDOWN function to round to the nearest two decimal places for -1.231, what will you get?
-1.23

20. What issue can you run into if you use ROUNDUP or ROUNDDOWN instead of ROUND?

It creates a small bias to always round in just one direction. If you use ROUND and the results are randomly distributed, then over time your rounding up and rounding down will balance out to a net result very close to zero. But if you always round up or always round down then over time as you do so more and more the total result will move more and more from the true result.

BASIC COUNT FUNCTIONS QUIZ
ANSWERS

1. What does the COUNT function allow you to do?
It allows you to count how many cells within the specified range have a number or date in them.

2. Does COUNT include cells with text in them?
No.

3. Does COUNT include cells with formulas in them that create a number or date?
Yes.

4. Does COUNT include cells with formulas in them that create a text entry?
No.

5. If a cell contains "1 unit" as its value, will COUNT count it?
No.

6. How would you use COUNT on a range of cells from B2 through D8?

=COUNT(B2:D8)

7. What function can you use if you also want to count cells that contain text in them?

COUNTA

8. What does this function allow you to do?

Count all cells in the range that are not empty.

9. What happens when you have a function in a cell, say =CONCATENATE(A1,B1,C1) but that cell is currently not displaying a value and you use each of the count functions?

COUNT will not count the cell. COUNTA will.

10. What should you always do when using any function?

Test to make sure that it's doing what you think it should be, including testing the COUNT functions to make sure that the cells you want counted are being counted.

11. What does COUNTBLANK do?

It counts the number of cells in the range that are empty. That means any cells that would return a value of "" but not cells with zero values or spaces in them.

12. If you have an issue with which cells are being counted by a specific count function, what should you do?

Look to the nature of the cells in question. Perhaps they look blank but have a space in them or they look blank but contain a function.

THE COUNTIFS, SUMIFS, AND AVERAGEIFS FUNCTIONS QUIZ ANSWERS

1. What is the difference between COUNTIFS, SUMIFS, and AVERAGEIFS?

COUNTIFS will count the number of entries that meet your specified criteria. SUMIFS will sum the values in a specified range of cells when your specified criteria are met. AVERAGEIFS will average the values in a specified range of cells when your specified criteria are met.

2. If you have access to both COUNTIF and COUNTIFS (or both SUMIF and SUMIFS, or both AVERAGEIF and AVERAGEIFS), which one should you use? Why?

Use the COUNTIFS, SUMIFS, or AVERAGEIFS versions because they can do everything their counterpart (COUNTIF, SUMIF, or AVERAGEIF) can do as well as handle multiple criteria. And since the order of the inputs is different, at least with SUMIFS and AVERAGEIFS, it's better to just always work with the more recent version of the function.

3. What is the difference between COUNTIF and COUNTIFS? What about SUMIF and SUMIFS? And AVERAGEIF and AVERAGEIFS?

COUNTIF can handle one criteria. COUNTIFS can handle multiple criteria. Same with the singular versions, SUMIF and AVERAGEIF, versus the plural versions, SUMIFS and AVERAGEIFS.

4. If you want to count how many times the values in Cells C10 through C25 are the same as the value in Cell A1, how would you write that function?

=COUNTIFS(C10:C25,A1)
or
=COUNTIF(C10:C25,A1)

5. What if you wanted to count how many times the cells in that range had text that included an e in it?

=COUNTIFS(C10:C25,"*e*")
or
=COUNTIF(C10:C25,"*e*")

6. Could you count how many cells from Cells C10 through C25 have the same values as Cell A1 AND how many have an e in them? If so, how would you write that and what issue would you potentially run into?

You could, but you'd have to use two COUNTIFS functions to do it and if it turned out the value in Cell A1 had an e in it, you could end up double-counting cells because you had to use two COUNTIFS functions.

=COUNTIFS(C10:C23,A1)+COUNTIFS(C10:C23,"*e*")
or
=COUNTIF(C10:C23,A1)+ COUNTIF(C10:C23,"*e*")

7. If you want to count how many times the values in Cells C10 through C25 are greater than the value in Cell A1, how would you write that?

=COUNTIFS(C10:C25,">"&A1)
or
=COUNTIF(C10:C25,">"&A1)

8. If you want to count how many customers are from Alaska and have bought Widgets when your customer location is stored in Column C and your product is stored in Column E, how would you write that?

=COUNTIFS(C:C,"Alaska",E:E,"Widgets")

9. If you want to count how many customers have bought more than 10 of your product and are from Hawaii when customer location is stored in Column C and number of units is in Column D, how would you write that?

=COUNTIFS(C:C,"Hawaii",D:D,">10")

10. If you want to count how many times Student A scored over 90 and Student B scored over 90 when their test scores are recorded in Rows 2 and 3, how would you do that?

=COUNTIFS(2:2,">90",3:3,">90")

11. What do you need to watch out for when using COUNTIFS, SUMIFS, and AVERAGEIFS?
    That your cell ranges for each of your criteria are properly lined up. If your data is stored across columns then you want to make sure your data starts with the same row number for all criteria, for example, so that Excel is looking at the values for the criteria in those columns

across the same row. (Assuming that's how your data is set up. As long as the cell ranges are the same size, Excel can work with it, but remember, garbage in, garbage out.)

12. If you want to total the value of all customer orders, which is listed in Column H, for all customers from Maine, which is listed in Column C, and who bought Widgets, which is listed in Column E, how would you do that?

=SUMIFS(H:H,C:C,"Maine",E:E,"Widgets")

13. Can you total the value of all customer orders over $100 using SUMIF or SUMIFS? How would you write that assuming customer order value is listed in Column H?
Yes.
=SUMIF(H:H,">100")
or
=SUMIFS(H:H,H:H,">100")

14. What do the asterisk (*), the question mark (?), and the tilde (~) represent when you're writing a count, sum, or average criteria?
The asterisk is a wildcard that represents any number of characters. The question mark is a wildcard that represents one single character. The tilde is a symbol you can use before an asterisk or question mark to indicate that that's actually what you wanted to search for rather than it being a wild card.

15. Can you calculate the average customer order for a customer in Colorado who made a purchase in June, assuming that customer order is stored in Column H, customer location is in Column C, and purchase month is in Column B? How would you write that?
Yes.

=AVERAGEIFS(H:H,C:C,"Colorado",B:B,"June")

16. If there are no customer transactions that meet that criteria what result is Excel going to return?
#DIV/0!

17. With COUNTIFS, SUMIFS, and AVERAGEIFS, if you have three criteria you specify and two of the three are met, what will happen with that entry?
It will not be included in the calculation. All of the criteria you specify must be met for Excel to count the entry or include its value in the sum or average calculation.

18. Why is this important?
Because if you write one of your criteria wrong, your function is not going to work properly. Remember to test, test, test your function, especially along the borders. So if your criteria is all entries over 100, test 101 and 100 to see what result you get.

BASIC TEXT FUNCTIONS
QUIZ ANSWERS

1. If you want to convert a text string into uppercase letters, which function should you use?

UPPER

2. What if you want to convert a text string into lowercase letters?

LOWER

3. What if you want the initial letter of each word to be capitalized, but the rest to be in lowercase?

PROPER

4. Let's say that you have a text string in Cell C10 and another in Cell C11 and that you want to combine those entries with a space between them and convert them into uppercase letters. How could you do that?

Once solution would be:

=UPPER(CONCATENATE(C10," ",C11))

5. What does CONCATENATE do?

Allows you to join several "text" strings into one. Text strings can be cell references or actual text that you input, including spaces and symbols.

6. What is the difference between proper case and title case?

Proper case capitalizes the first letter of every single word. Title case capitalizes the first letter of significant words but does not capitalize smaller filler words like of, or, the, and, etc.

7. What does the LEFT function do?

It returns the first x number of characters from the left-hand side of a text string.

8. If you want to return the first five characters of the text in Cell A1, how would you do that?

=LEFT(A1,5)

9. Does this function work with numbers as well?

Yes.

10. What happens if the number of characters you specify is greater than the number of characters in the string you reference?

Excel returns the entire result.

11. What happens if you don't specify a number of characters to return?

Excel will default to a value of 1 and just return the first character.

12. For languages that don't work with characters, like Chinese, Japanese, and Korean, which function will do the same for those languages?

LEFTB

13. If you want to return the last two characters of a text string, how can you do that?

Using the RIGHT function.

14. What does the MID function do?

It returns the specified number of characters from a text string given a starting position. So if you tell it to go three characters in and then return the next three characters, it can do that.

15. What happens if the start point you provide for the MID function is greater than the number of characters in the string?

Excel returns an empty result.

16. What happens if you use MID and ask Excel to return more characters than there are in the text string?

It will return what there is.

17. What other function could you use to get the same result as =MID(A1,1,2)?

=LEFT(A1,2)

18. If you want to take a text string and remove all spaces from it except for one space between each word, which function can you use to do that?

TRIM

19. If you had a list of entries with first name, middle name, and last name in separate columns, Columns A, B, and C, and you wanted to combine those entries for each row into one entry with only one space between each word, and you knew that not every entry had a middle name, how could you use two functions to do that in one cell? Write the function for Row 1.

=TRIM(CONCATENATE(A1," ",B1," ",C1))

20. What do you need to be careful of when using any

of the above functions? What can you do when you're done with your manipulation to address this?

Your text entry is still a formula, meaning that if you change the values in the input cells (by, for example, deleting them) you will change the result of your formula. This is why it's a good idea once you're done with manipulating your text strings to copy and paste special-values to lock in the result as a text entry and remove the formulas. (But only do that when you're done and don't expect the inputs to change further.)

21. What type of inputs will CONCATENATE accept? And how do they need to be written?

Cell references, numbers, or text. Cell references can be written as they are (B1). Numbers can be written as they are or in quotes (32 or "32"). Text must be written in quotes ("text").

22. If you want there to be a space or a comma in your final CONCATENATE result, how do you do that?

Make it a text element in your function. So for that text element start with a quote mark and then add your space and/or comma and then close with a quote mark. Each text element in a CONCATENATE function is separated by a comma. For example, to create Jones, Albert where Jones was in Cell B1 and Albert was in Cell A1, you could write =CONCATENATE(B1,", ",A1) where the ", " is the second text element in the formula.

23. With CONCATENATE if you get a NAME#? error, what has generally gone wrong?

You likely failed to put quotation marks around a text element.

24. What function is Excel replacing CONCATENATE with?

CONCAT. It's in versions of Excel from 2016 onward.

THE TEXT FUNCTION
QUIZ ANSWERS

1. What does Excel say that the TEXT function can do?
Convert a value to text in a specific number format.

2. What else can the TEXT function actually do?
Extract information from a date. You can use TEXT to return the day of the week, month of the year, or a time component from a date. And with day of the week or month of the year that can be the written form of the date, so December or Dec, for example.

3. If you have a date in Cell A1 and want to pull the full name of the day of the week, how would you do that using the TEXT function?
=TEXT(A1,"dddd")

4. What about the month of the year?
=TEXT(A1,"mmmm")

5. If you use TEXT to create number formats, for example =TEXT(A1,"$0.00"), what issue can you run into?

Sometimes Excel will create numbers you never wanted. For example, if you use the wrong characters, you can end up with a whole number followed by a decimal with no numbers after the decimal (5.). Or you can end up with a whole number followed by a decimal followed by a space followed by another number (5. 1). Try, for example, =TEXT(5,"$?.??) to see what I mean.

6. What is the other thing to be aware of when using the TEXT function with a number?

It converts your entry into text, so it's no longer treated as a number by Excel. This means you can't do calculations on it anymore.

7. What's one quick way to see valid number formats you can use with the TEXT function?

Right-click on a cell, choose Format Cells, go to the Number tab, and choose Custom. You'll see a number of options there for how to format numbers that you can translate to the TEXT function. Excel won't accept all of them for the TEXT function, but it is a good start.

8. If you wanted to return the number value in Cell A1 as "50% Win Rate", how could you do that using TEXT?

=TEXT(A1,"00.00%")&" Win Rate" (Note that *50 Useful Functions* has an error in the text for this one. A1 would need to be .5 for this to return a value of 50% not 50 like the book says.)

THE TODAY AND NOW
FUNCTIONS QUIZ ANSWERS

1. What does the TODAY function do?

Returns the current date formatted as a date.

2. How do you write it?

=TODAY()

3. Why would you use it?

Because it helps as part of a calculation that's looking at how many days from today something needs to happen or did happen. For example, days past due on payment.

4. If you wanted to calculate how many days it's been since someone purchased your product, which is the better option: have a cell that uses =TODAY() and then another cell that calculates days since purchase or just have a cell that calculates days since purchase and incorporates TODAY() into the formula? Why?

It's better to have the TODAY() function in its own cell so that all assumptions are visible. This way you can confirm that the worksheet updated. when you opened it.

Also, there will be times when someone isn't expecting the worksheet to have updated so having that visible makes it obvious what's happened.

5. What does the NOW function do?

Returns the current date *and time* formatted as a date and time.

6. What's the difference between using TODAY and NOW?

TODAY will return today's date with a time of midnight. NOW will return today's date with the current time.

7. Why does this matter?

Because if you intend to use formulas to calculate differences between two times and it doesn't matter to you that that calculation be accurate down to the minute, you should be using TODAY instead of NOW.

8. What do you need to be aware of when using both TODAY and NOW?

That they update whenever you open your worksheet, when you press F9, and when you do any other calculation in your worksheet. So if you need to capture the time right now and then preserve that value, you'll need to take steps to replace that value with a fixed value instead of a function.

9. How does Excel treat dates for the purpose of addition and subtraction?

It converts the hours for a day into a decimal. So 12 hours is equivalent to .5 since it's half a day. The number 5 would represent 5 whole days.

10. So if you wanted to calculate the date five and a half days from today's date, what could you use?

=TODAY()+5.5

11. What if you wanted to calculate the date and time exactly five and a half days from this moment?
=NOW()+5.5

12. Is it possible that those two formulas could return different dates?
Yes.

THE IF FUNCTION
QUIZ ANSWERS

1. What does an IF function do?

It allows you to return different results depending on whether the criteria you specify are met or not.

2. Translate the IF function =IF(A2>25,0,A2*0.05) into a written description.

IF Cell A2 has a value greater than 25 then return a value of zero. Otherwise, return a value equal to the value in Cell A2 times .05.

3. What is another way to think about the components of an IF function?

IF(If, Then, Else) or IF A, THEN B, ELSE C or IF A, THEN B, OTHERWISE C.

4. What does it mean that you can nest IF functions?

It means that you can start with one IF function and then replace either the THEN component or the ELSE component with another IF function so that you get IF A, THEN B, ELSE, IF C, THEN D, OTHERWISE E, for example.

5. If you're going to nest IF functions, which is it better to replace, the Then portion or the Else portion? Why?

The Else portion. Because then that keeps all of the parts of each individual IF function together as opposed to splitting them up across the function.

6. Translate the IF function =IF(A9>$A$5,$B$5,IF (A9>$A$4,$B$4,0)) into a written description.

If the value in Cell A9 is greater than the value in Cell A5, then return the value in Cell B5. Otherwise, if the value in Cell A9 is greater than the value in Cell A4, return the value in Cell B4. Otherwise return a value of zero.

7. If you were to copy the above formula into a new cell, how would it change?

The only thing that would change is the cell reference to cell A9, the rest of the function uses $ signs to refer to specified cells. It's using a table to generate the results of the IF function.

8. If you have a long and complex nested IF function that you can't get to work, what are some ways you can troubleshoot the IF function to figure out what's wrong?

Arrow through the function to make sure that you have the correct number of opening and closing parens. For each IF in the function there should be one opening paren immediately after the IF and a corresponding closing paren somewhere in the function.

Replace all but one of the IF functions with a placeholder result to create a simple IF function and evaluate whether it's doing what it should. So, for example,

=IF(A9>$A$5,$B$5,IF(A9>$A$4,$B$4,0))

would become

=IF(A9>$A$5,$B$5,"ELSE")

where the second IF function has temporarily been replaced with a result of ELSE.

9. What is the most likely issue if Excel tells you you've entered too many arguments with an IF function?

You probably have a misplaced paren somewhere. (Older versions of Excel did limit the number of IF functions you could nest, but in current versions you're unlikely to have too many IF functions nested.)

10. What should you always do with an IF function that you create? (Or any function really?)

Test it to make sure it's doing what it should be. Pay particular attention to threshold results where the result should transition from one result to another. For example, did you mean greater than or did you mean greater than or equal to and how did you actually write it?

11. If you write an IF function that's referencing a table of fixed values (like a discount table) what should you always be sure to do?

Use $ signs when writing the references to those cells so that you can easily copy your IF function while keeping the table references fixed.

VLOOKUP QUIZ ANSWERS

1. What does VLOOKUP do?

Looks for a value in the leftmost column of a cell range and then returns a value in the same row for a column you specify.

2. What must you do if you're using VLOOKUP on a table?

Sort your data using the values in that first column.

3. What's the best use for VLOOKUP?

Finding values in a reference table that's built to be used with the function.

4. Do the values in a reference table need to be an exact match for the value you're looking for for VLOOKUP to work?

No.

5. What is the minimum number of columns your data needs for VLOOKUP to work?

One. You can use VLOOKUP to look up the closest value to your lookup value.

6. Can the column that has the values you're looking up be located anywhere in your data?

No. It must be the left-most column in the range you specify. It doesn't have to be the left-most column in your data but it must be the left-most column in the range and it must be to the left of the column with the values you want to return.

7. How do you tell Excel whether to look for an exact match or an approximate match?

With the fourth element of your function. If you say TRUE or 1, it will look for an approximate match. If you say FALSE or 0, it will look for an exact match only.

8. What is the difference between an exact match and an approximate match?

An exact match will only return a result when what you're looking for is an exact match to an entry in the data table. An approximate match will return a result that's closest to the value you're looking for.

9. What is =VLOOKUP(25,A1:E10,3,FALSE) saying to do?

Lookup the value of 25 in Column A of a cell range that starts in Cell A1 and ends in Cell E10. If there is a value of 25 in the that column then return the value in the row that contains the value of 25 from Column C.

10. What is =VLOOKUP(25,A1:E10,2,TRUE) saying to do?

Lookup the value of 25 in Column A of a cell range that starts in Cell A1 and ends in Cell E10. Find the row in Column A of the table that is either equal to 25 or directly before the first row that has a value of more than 25 and return the value in Column B of that row.

11. What do you need to be careful of when using VLOOKUP with apparent numbers or dates?

If the numbers or dates are stored as text, they may produce unexpected results.

12. What should you always do when using any function in Excel?

Test to make sure that the result you get makes sense.

THE AND & OR FUNCTIONS
QUIZ ANSWERS

1. What does the AND function do?

Checks to see if all arguments are true or not. If so, it returns TRUE. If not, it returns FALSE.

2. What does the OR function do?

Checks to see if any of the arguments listed are true. If so, it returns TRUE. If not, it returns FALSE.

3. What is =AND(A1>5,A2>4) asking?

Is it true that the value in A1 is greater than five and that the value in A2 is greater than 4?

4. What is =OR(A1>5,A2>4) asking?

Is either the value in A1 greater than five or the value in A2 greater than 4?

5. What is =AND(A1>B1,A2>B2) asking?

Is the value in A1 greater than the value in B1 and is the value in A2 greater than B2.

6. What is =IF(AND(A1="Jones",B1="Whatsit"), C1,D1) doing?

It's saying that if the value in Cell A1 is Jones and the value in B1 is Whatsit then return the value in C1, otherwise return the value in D1.

7. What is =IF(OR(A1="Canton",B1="Toledo"), G1,G1*2) doing?

It's saying that if the value in Cell A1 is either Canton or Toledo then return the value in G1. If it isn't, then return a value of G1 times two.

THE TRUE, FALSE AND NA
FUNCTIONS QUIZ ANSWERS

1. What do the TRUE and FALSE functions do?
They return a value of TRUE or FALSE.

2. When might you use them?
When you're using functions that return different results for a TRUE or FALSE result. Sometimes simply typing TRUE or FALSE doesn't create the same result as using TRUE() and FALSE() the functions. For example, say you wanted to use AVERAGEA on the results of an IF function. You could have the IF function return a result of TRUE or FALSE and then apply AVERAGEA to those results.

3. What does the NA function do?
Returns the error value #N/A.

4. When might you use the NA function?
To mark empty cells when using a formula. If you return an empty space instead of an N/A result some functions won't work properly. This can be especially useful when

having to graph results since Excel will skip N/A values whereas it will not skip empty results.

5. What do you need to remember when using the TRUE, FALSE, or NA functions?

That you always need to include the parens after the function name. So write TRUE() not TRUE.

RANDOM NUMBERS
QUIZ ANSWERS

1. What function will return a random number greater than or equal to 0 and less than 1 evenly distributed?
RAND

2. What function will return a random whole number between two values you specify?
RANDBETWEEN

3. If I want to return any possible value, including a decimal value between 0 and 100, how can I do that?
=100*RAND()

4. If I want to return any whole number between 0 and 100, how can I do that?
=RANDBETWEEN(0,100) or =INT(RAND()*100)

5. What do you need to be careful of when using either function?
It will generate a new random value every time you recalculate your worksheet with F9, every time you do

another calculation in your worksheet, and every time you open the worksheet and you won't be able to go back to the previously-generated value.

6. How can you work around this if you need to capture that value?

Generate your random value and then use copy and paste special-values to convert the entry to a value instead of keep it as a function.

RANKING QUIZ ANSWERS

1. What function or functions can you use if you want to know the rank of a specific value within a range of possible values? In other words, is this the 5ᵗʰ largest number, the 10ᵗʰ, the 20ᵗʰ, etc. compared to other numbers in the range?

RANK, RANK.EQ, or RANK.AVG

2. If you want to know the rank of a value in Cell A1 from within the range of Cells A1 through A15, how can you write that function using ascending values?

=RANK(A1,A1:A15,1)
or
=RANK.EQ(A1,A1:A15,1)
or
=RANK.AVG(A1,A1:A15,1)

3. What about using descending values?

=RANK(A1,A1:A15,0)
or

=RANK(A1,A1:A15)
or
=RANK.EQ(A1,A1:A15)
or
=RANK.AVG(A1,A1:A15)

4. To use the functions does your data have to be sorted?

No.

5. What happens if you use RANK on a data set where there are multiples of a value?

All instances of that value are assigned the same rank and then Excel skips however many ranks it needs to to account for that. So you can end up with ranks of 1, 2, 2, 2, and 5 for a dataset that has the values 2, 3, 3, 3, and 4.

6. How do RANK.EQ and RANK.AVG differ?

In how they treat instances where there is more than one of a result. For RANK.EQ it works like RANK and all ties are assigned the highest possible rank for that value and then Excel skips however many ranks it needs to. For RANK.AVG Excel takes the possible ranks for those tied values and returns an average for the ranks. (See the guide for a detailed discussion of how this works.)

THE SMALL AND LARGE
FUNCTIONS QUIZ ANSWERS

1. What does the SMALL function do?

Returns the k-th smallest value in a data set where you specify the value of k.

2. What does the LARGE function do?

Returns the k-th largest value in a data set where you specify the value of k.

3. Can you technically use SMALL to return the largest value in a range and LARGE to return the smallest value in a range?

Yes. As long as you know the size of your range and use a k that's equal to that number.

4. What does the ROWS function do?

It counts the number of rows in your selection.

COMBINING FUNCTIONS QUIZ ANSWERS

1. Is it possible to write a formula that uses more than one function?

Absolutely.

2. How would you write a formula that returns a value of TRUE if the value in Cell A1 is greater than 10 or the value in Cell B1 is greater than 10 and a value of FALSE otherwise?

=IF(OR(A1>10,B1>10),TRUE(),FALSE())

Note that that used four different functions in one formula.

3. What do you need to be careful about when combining functions together in one formula?

That you have all of your parens in the right place and don't forget any.

4. Do you need to use an equals sign in front of each function name when you combine functions in a single formula?

No. You just need to start your formula with an equals sign, but that's it.

5. What should you explore further if you're running into file size issues because of repeat calculations in your Excel worksheet?

Array formulas.

WHEN THINGS GO WRONG
QUIZ ANSWERS

1. Name five different error messages you might see.

#REF!, #VALUE!, #DIV/0!, #N/A, #NUM!

You also might see a comment that you've created a circular references or have too few arguments or that the formula you've written doesn't work and Excel wants to fix it for you.

2. What does #REF! generally indicate?

That you've deleted a value that was being referenced in that cell. For example, =A1+B1 will generate that message if you delete Column A or Column B.

3. How can you see where the cell that was deleted was located in your formula?

Click on the cell and look in the formula bar or double-click on the cell. The cell reference that's missing will have been replaced with #REF!.

4. What does a #VALUE! message indicate?

That the cell you're referencing is the wrong type of cell for that function. So maybe you have a date or number formatted as plain text, for example. In rare cases it could also mean that you have regional settings that impact how you're supposed to write your functions. It can also mean that you're referencing a now unavailable outside data source.

5. What does a #DIV/0! message indicate?

That you're dividing by zero or a blank cell.

6. If the #DIV/0! message is legitimate because nothing has been entered yet, what's a quick way to suppress it?

Use an IF function in that cell rather than just a division formula. So instead of having =A1/B1, have =IF(B1<>0,A1/B1,"").

7. What does a #N/A error message generally mean?

That Excel isn't finding what it was asked to look for.

8. What can you check for if this happens and you don't think it should have?

Check the formatting of your values to make sure they match. Also check that there aren't extra spaces in one of your inputs or lookup values.

9. What does the IFERROR function do? What do you need to be careful with if you use it?

Suppresses an error result and replaces it with a zero, a blank space, or text that you provide. It will suppress all error messages, even ones you may want to see.

10. What does the #NUM! error message generally indicate?

That there are numeric values in a function that are not valid. It also happens when the function is going to return a result that is too large or too small or can't find a solution.

11. What is a circular reference?

One that references itself. So if in Cell A1 I write =A1+B1 that is circular because to generate the answer in Cell A1 I would have to use the value in Cell A1. That would create a continuous loop if you actually tried to do it.

12. If you don't think you have a circular reference but Excel tells you you do, what should you check for?

That you haven't created an indirect circular reference. For example, if you write in Cell A1 =B1+C1 that looks fine. But if the value in C1 is calculated by =SUM(A:A) then you're using the value in Cell A1 to calculate the value in Cell C1 and can't also use it to calculate the value in Cell A1.

13. If you're trying to figure out what cells are feeding the value in a cell where can you go to do that?

Trace Precedents under Formula Auditing in the Formulas tab.

14. If Excel tells you you have too few arguments, what should you check for?

First, that you've included all required inputs for that particular function. In the function description anything listed with brackets is optional, but anything listed as text without brackets is not. Also, check that you have all of your parens and commas and quotation marks in the right places.

15. What can you do with a formula that just isn't working the way it should be?

Double-click on the formula and check that all of the cell references are pointing to the right cells. Also, if you're copying a formula make sure that you used $ signs to lock any cell references that need to be locked. Also make sure that any options for that function were chosen properly. (Exact versus approximate, ascending vs. descending, etc.)

(And one that isn't in the guide, but came up as I was writing this, if you copied from Word into Excel make sure that you replace any curly quotes or smart quotes with straight quotes. Excel will not accept smart quotes.)

CELL NOTATION
QUIZ ANSWERS

1. What is Cell A1 referencing?
The cell that's in Column A and Row 1.

2. Name two ways you can reference more than one cell in a function.
With a comma between individual cells, row references, or column references. Or with a colon to reference a range of cells, rows, or columns.

For example:
=SUM(A1, B1, C1)
or
=SUM(A:A,B:B,C:C)
or
=SUM(1:1,2:2,3:3)
or
=SUM(A1:C1)
or
=SUM(A:C)
or
=SUM(1:3)

3. Can you reference a cell in another worksheet?

Yes. You just need to include the worksheet name reference as well.

4. Can you reference a cell in another workbook?

Yes. You just need to include the workbook name reference as well, but be careful doing so because the formula may not work if that other workbook is moved, renamed, or deleted.

5. What's an easy way to reference a cell in another worksheet or workbook?

Start your formula and then just click on the cell you need. Excel will write the cell reference for you.

BONUS:
EXERCISES

EXERCISE 1

Take the following data and calculate

	A	B	C	D
1	**Customer Name**	**Units**	**Price**	**Product**
2	Albert Jones	5	$2.50	Widgets
3	Mark Smith	10	$5.00	Whatsits
4	Nancy Baker	5	$2.50	Whatsits
5	Albert Jones	10	$5.00	Whatsits
6	Mark Smith	5	$5.00	Whatsits
7	Nancy Baker	5	$5.00	Whatsits
8	Albert Jones	4	$5.00	Widgets
9	Mark Smith	3	$2.50	Widgets
10	Nancy Baker	2	$2.50	Widgets

1. The total spent for each transaction.

2. The total number of units sold.

3. The total amount earned using SUMPRODUCT.

4. The average price per unit across the transactions.

5. Build a grid from that data that has customer name in rows and product across the top and calculate:
 A. Amount spent per customer per product.
 B. Number of units ordered per customer per product.
 C. Average unit price paid per transaction per customer per product.

EXERCISE 2

1. Take the following numbers and calculate the average, median, and mode.

2. Also calculate the mode.mult with room for four possible results.

10

10

10

20

50

300

300

300

40

50

1200

1200

1200

50

EXERCISE 3

Take the following data table and combine the entries to form a single entry with last name, first name middle name for each row with no additional spaces and the name in all caps. Do this in one formula for each entry.

	A	B	C
1	**First Name**	**Middle Name**	**Last Name**
2	Amanda	Diane	Cook
3	Mark	David	Allen
4	Brad		Jones
5	Alejandro		Sanchez

EXERCISE 4

1. Build a simple discount table that gives customers $5 off if they spend $25 or more and $10 off if they spend $50 or more and then write a VLOOKUP function to find the discount for purchases of $5, $25, $45, $50, and $75.

2. Do the same with a nested IF function.

EXERCISE 5

Using the following numbers answer the following questions:

10

12

14

5

8

7

16

20

22

34

1. Looking from smallest value to largest value, what place in the order is 8?

2. Looking from largest value to smallest value, what place in the order is 22?

3. What value is the 6th smallest value?

4. What value is the 4th largest value?

5. How could you calculate a random whole number that is between the smallest value in this range and the largest value in this range using one formula to calculate the smallest and largest value as well as the random number?

BONUS:
EXERCISE ANSWERS

EXERCISE 1

Take the following data and calculate

	A	B	C	D
1	**Customer Name**	**Units**	**Price**	**Product**
2	Albert Jones	5	$2.50	Widgets
3	Mark Smith	10	$5.00	Whatsits
4	Nancy Baker	5	$2.50	Whatsits
5	Albert Jones	10	$5.00	Whatsits
6	Mark Smith	5	$5.00	Whatsits
7	Nancy Baker	5	$5.00	Whatsits
8	Albert Jones	4	$5.00	Widgets
9	Mark Smith	3	$2.50	Widgets
10	Nancy Baker	2	$2.50	Widgets

1. The total spent for each transaction.

2. The total number of units sold.

3. The total amount earned using SUMPRODUCT.

4. The average price per unit across the transactions.

5. Build a grid from that data that has customer name in rows and product across the top and calculate:

A. Amount spent per customer per product.

B. Number of units ordered per customer per product.

C. Average unit price paid per transaction per customer per product.

* * *

	A	B	C	D	E
1	**Customer Name**	**Units**	**Price**	**Product**	**Total Sper**
2	Albert Jones	5	$2.50	Widgets	$12.50
3	Mark Smith	10	$5.00	Whatsits	$50.00
4	Nancy Baker	5	$2.50	Whatsits	$12.50
5	Albert Jones	10	$5.00	Whatsits	$50.00
6	Mark Smith	5	$5.00	Whatsits	$25.00
7	Nancy Baker	5	$5.00	Whatsits	$25.00
8	Albert Jones	4	$5.00	Widgets	$20.00
9	Mark Smith	3	$2.50	Widgets	$7.50
10	Nancy Baker	2	$2.50	Widgets	$5.00
11	**Total**	**49**			**$207.50**
12					
13					
14	Avg Price Per Unit Per Trans	$3.89		SUMPRODUCT	$207.50
15					

1. The total spent for each transaction.

Formula for Cell E2 is

=B2*C2

This can be copied down to the rest of the rows in the table.

2. The total number of units sold.

Formula in B11 is

=SUM(B2:B10)

This can also be created using the AutoSum option.

3. The total amount earned using SUMPRODUCT.
The formula to calculate the total amount earned using SUMPRODUCT is

=SUMPRODUCT(B2:B10,C2:C10)

4. The average price per unit across the transactions.
To calculate the average of the per unit prices paid across the transaction you can use the formula:

=AVERAGE(C2:C10)

5. Build a grid from that data that has customer name in rows and product across the top and calculate:

	H	I	J
1	**Amount Spent**	Whatsits	Widgets
2	Albert Jones	$ 50.00	$ 32.50
3	Mark Smith	$ 75.00	$ 7.50
4	Nancy Baker	$ 37.50	$ 5.00
5			
6	**Units Ordered**	Whatsits	Widgets
7	Albert Jones	10	9
8	Mark Smith	15	3
9	Nancy Baker	10	2
10			
11	**Average Unit Price**	Whatsits	Widgets
12	Albert Jones	$5.00	$3.75
13	Mark Smith	$5.00	$2.50
14	Nancy Baker	$3.75	$2.50

A. Amount spent per customer per product.

Assuming customer name is in Column H and product is in Row 1 as shown in the solution above, in Cell I2 write the formula

=SUMIFS($E:$E,$A:$A,$H2,$D:D,I1)

and then copy it to the rest of the cells in the table.

B. Number of units ordered per customer per product.

Assuming customer name is in Column H and product is in Row 6 as shown in the solution above, in Cell I7 write the formula

=SUMIFS($B:$B,$A:$A,$H7,$D:D,I6)

and then copy it to the rest of the cells in the table.

C. Average unit price paid per transaction per customer per product.

Assuming customer name is in Column H and product is in Row 11 as shown in the solution above, in Cell I12 write the formula

=AVERAGEIFS($C:$C,$A:$A,$H12,$D:D,I11)

and then copy it to the rest of the cells in the table.

EXERCISE 2

1. Take the following numbers and calculate the average, median, and mode.

2. Also calculate the mode.mult with room for four possible results.

10

10

10

20

50

300

300

300

40

50

1200

1200

1200

50

* * *

	A	B	C	D
1	10			
2	10		Average	338.5714
3	10		Median	50
4	20		Mode	10
5	50			10
6	300			50
7	300		Mode.Mult	300
8	300			1200
9	40			
10	50			
11	1200			
12	1200			
13	1200			
14	50			

1. To calculate the average, median, and mode with the values in Cells A1 through A14 use:

=AVERAGE(A1:A14)

=MEDIAN(A1:A14)

=MODE(A1:A14)

2. To calculate the multiple mode outcome:

A. Select Cells D5 through D8

B. Use =MODE.MULT(A1:A14)

C. Finish with Ctrl + Shift + Enter rather than enter.

EXERCISE 3

Take the following data table and combine the entries to form a single entry with last name, first name middle name for each row with no additional spaces and the name in all caps. Do this in one formula for each entry.

	A	B	C
1	**First Name**	**Middle Name**	**Last Name**
2	Amanda	Diane	Cook
3	Mark	David	Allen
4	Brad		Jones
5	Alejandro		Sanchez

* * *

	A	B	C	D
1	First Name	Middle Name	Last Name	Last, First Middle
2	Amanda	Diane	Cook	COOK, AMANDA DIANE
3	Mark	David	Allen	ALLEN, MARK DAVID
4	Brad		Jones	JONES, BRAD
5	Alejandro		Sanchez	SANCHEZ, ALEJANDRO

One way to do this is to use the formula

=UPPER(TRIM(CONCATENATE(C2,", ",A2," ",B2)))

You could also do it with the TRIM and UPPER functions in different positions within the formula.

EXERCISE 4

1. Build a simple discount table that gives customers $5 off if they spend $25 or more and $10 off if they spend $50 or more and then write a VLOOKUP function to find the discount for purchases of $5, $25, $45, $50, and $75.

2. Do the same with a nested IF function.

* * *

Here is one possible way to structure the problem:

A. Build a discount table in Cells A1 through B5 with the values in Cells A3 through B5.

B. Place the test values in Cells A8 through A12.

	A	B	C	D
1	**Discount Table**			
2	**Purchase Amount**	**Discount**		
3	$0.00	$0.00		
4	$25.00	$5.00		
5	$50.00	$10.00		
6				
7	**Test Amounts**	**VLOOKUP**	**IF Function**	
8	$5.00	$0.00	$0.00	
9	$25.00	$5.00	$5.00	
10	$45.00	$5.00	$5.00	
11	$50.00	$10.00	$10.00	
12	$75.00	$10.00	$10.00	
13				
14	**Row 8 Formulas**			
15	**VLOOKUP**	=VLOOKUP(A8,$A$3:$B$5,2)		
16	**IF Function**	=IF(A8<$A$4,$B$3,IF(A8<$A$5,$B$4,$B$5))		

1. In Row 8 for the VLOOKUP function you can then write the formula:

=VLOOKUP(A8,$A$3:$B$5,2)

and copy it down to the rest of the cells. Because of the $ signs in the formula it will continue to work for all rows.

2. In Row 8 for the IF function you can then write the formula:

=IF(A8<$A$4,$B$3,IF(A8<$A$5,$B$4,$B$5))

and copy that down to the rest of the cells and because of the $ signs it will also continue to work for all rows.

EXERCISE 5

Using the following numbers answer the following questions:

10
12
14
5
8
7
16
20
22
34

1. Looking from smallest value to largest value, what place in the order is 8?

2. Looking from largest value to smallest value, what place in the order is 22?

3. What value is the 6th smallest value?

4. What value is the 4th largest value?

5. How could you calculate a random whole number that is between the smallest value in this range and the largest value in this range using one formula to calculate the smallest and largest value as well as the random number?

* * *

The formulas given below assume you entered the values in Cells A1 through A10, but the results should be the same no matter where you entered the values.

1. Looking from smallest value to largest value, what place in the order is 8?

3rd. You can use =RANK(8,A1:A10,1) to calculate this.

2. Looking from largest value to smallest value, what place in the order is 22?

2nd. You can use =RANK(22,A1:A10) to calculate this.

3. What value is the 6th smallest value?

14. You can use =SMALL(A1:A10,6) to calculate this.

4. What value is the 4th largest value?

16. You can use =LARGE(A1:A10,4) to calculate this.

5. How could you calculate a random whole number that is between the smallest value in this range and the largest value in this range using one formula to calculate the smallest and largest value as well as the random number?

Using
=RANDBETWEEN(SMALL(A1:A10,1),LARGE(A1:A10,1))

INDEX OF QUIZZES

Quiz Name	Quiz	Answers
Ranking Quiz	49	123
The SMALL And LARGE Functions Quiz	51	125
Combining Functions Quiz	53	127
When Things Go Wrong (Functions) Quiz	55	129
Cell Notation Quiz	57	133

ABOUT THE AUTHOR

M.L. Humphrey is a former stockbroker with a degree in Economics from Stanford and an MBA from Wharton who has spent close to twenty years as a regulator and consultant in the financial services industry.

You can reach M.L. at mlhumphreywriter@gmail.com or at mlhumphrey.com.